REACHING INTO SPACE

Written by Barbara Reeves

MODERN CURRICULUM PRESS

PROJECT DIRECTOR: Susan Cornell Poskanzer
ART DIRECTOR: Lisa Olsson

 MODERN CURRICULUM PRESS
13900 Prospect Road, Cleveland, Ohio 44136
Simon & Schuster • A Paramount Communications Company

PHOTOGRAPHY CREDITS
Front Jacket: © NASA
© Celestron International inside covers; © NASA pp. 3, 4, 6, 7, 9-16, inside back cover logo;
© Wide World Photos, Inc. pp. 5, 8

ISBN 0-8136-1176-8 (STY PK)   ISBN 0-8136-1177-6 (BB)   ISBN 0-8136-1178-4 (SB)

10 9 8 7   00 99 98

The date was May 7, 1992. The place was Cape Canaveral, Florida. Waving and smiling, seven astronauts headed for a spaceship waiting on a launching pad. They were the crew of the Endeavour. They were about to take off on one of the greatest adventures of their lives.

MAY 7, 1992

3

At 7:40 P.M. the space shuttle Endeavour lifted off for the first time. It soared high into a partly cloudy sky. The adventure had begun.

7:40 P.M.

Once in space, one of the most important jobs was to rescue a satellite. The satellite was the Intelsat 6. It was launched in 1990. But it never reached the right orbit, or path, in space.

MAY 8, 1992

The crew planned to capture the satellite and to join it to a new rocket motor. They wanted to send the satellite into a higher orbit.

On May 10, two astronauts walked out into space. One astronaut, Commander Thout (THOO-it), wanted to grab the slowly turning satellite with a special bar. Then the astronauts could pull the satellite into the shuttle's cargo bay, or storage area. But the bar didn't work right. The astronauts had to leave the wobbling satellite in space.

The next day the astronauts tried for two hours to snag the satellite. They failed, but they wouldn't give up. People around the world were counting on them!

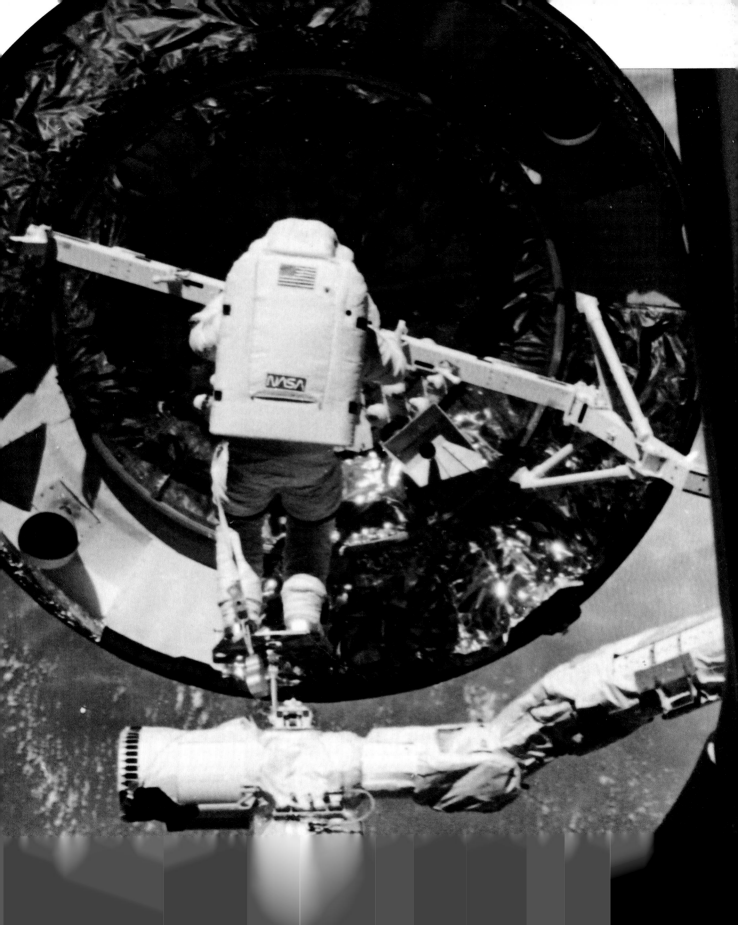

A thrilling rescue plan was set for May 13. On that day, the Endeavour moved very close to Intelsat 6. Then for the first time ever, three astronauts walked in space together. These daring astronauts tried to grab the satellite using only their gloved hands!

MAY 13, 1992

The astronauts had to be very careful. If their space suits ripped, they could be killed. If they pushed the satellite too hard, it would crash into the shuttle. Objects in space are weightless. But if they bump into each other, they can cause a lot of damage.

The astronauts worked for hours, floating 230 miles above Earth. Finally, they were successful.

"Houston, I think we've got a satellite," the shuttle commander radioed to Earth as they captured Intelsat 6.

Endeavour carried many space-age tools. But in the end the astronauts solved the tricky problem using only their own hands!

The astronauts joined the satellite to its new rocket motor. Later they set it free and blasted the satellite into a new orbit.

The next day, there was one more space walk. That time, only two astronauts went into the darkness of space. They practiced building part of a space station. They also tried out exciting ideas for space rescues.

Their work was important. Someday space-walking astronauts will build huge space stations in space. The astronauts on the Endeavour were helping to make this fantastic dream come true.

MAY 14, 1992

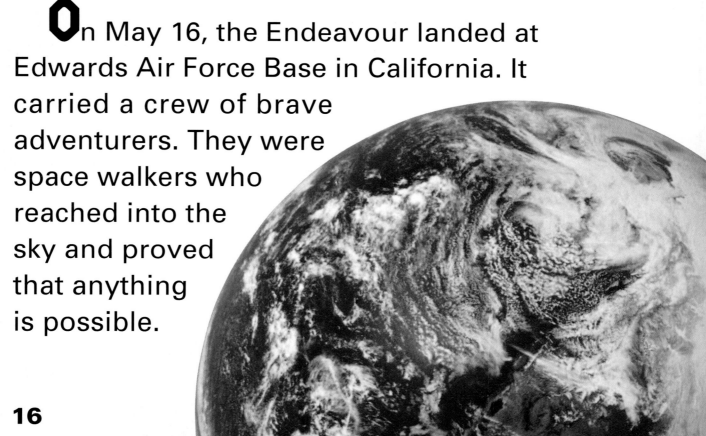

On May 16, the Endeavour landed at Edwards Air Force Base in California. It carried a crew of brave adventurers. They were space walkers who reached into the sky and proved that anything is possible.